NIBBANA
STREAM WINNER TO ARAHANTSHIP

THE MIDDLE WAY
GATEWAY TO SELF HELP

By

DR ARIYATHUSHEL ARAHANT

Chennai • Bangalore

CLEVER FOX PUBLISHING
Chennai, India

Published by CLEVER FOX PUBLISHING 2024
Copyright © Dr Ariyathushel Arahant 2024

All Rights Reserved.
ISBN: 978-93-56487-66-6

This book has been published with all reasonable efforts taken to make the material error-free after the consent of the author. No part of this book shall be used, reproduced in any manner whatsoever without written permission from the author, except in the case of brief quotations embodied in critical articles and reviews.

The Author of this book is solely responsible and liable for its content including but not limited to the views, representations, descriptions, statements, information, opinions and references ["Content"]. The Content of this book shall not constitute or be construed or deemed to reflect the opinion or expression of the Publisher or Editor. Neither the Publisher nor Editor endorse or approve the Content of this book or guarantee the reliability, accuracy or completeness of the Content published herein and do not make any representations or warranties of any kind, express or implied, including but not limited to the implied warranties of merchantability, fitness for a particular purpose. The Publisher and Editor shall not be liable whatsoever for any errors, omissions, whether such errors or omissions result from negligence, accident, or any other cause or claims for loss or damages of any kind, including without limitation, indirect or consequential loss or damage arising out of use, inability to use, or about the reliability, accuracy or sufficiency of the information contained in this book.

Homage to the Supremely Enlightened Buddha!

Certainly, Buddha's Dhamma leads to cessation, Nibbana across stages.
The knower of all worlds, the highest Jewel, the teacher of all perfected ones;
homage to the supremely enlightened Buddha!

Table of Contents

Preface 1
Chapter One: *The Journey to the Middle Way* 2
Chapter Two: *Stream of Thoughts* 4
Chapter Three: *Ordinary Ways of Thinking* 7
Chapter Four: *Understanding Emptiness* 11
Chapter Five: *Life Experiences* 18
Chapter Six: *Awakening* 20
Chapter Seven: *Thinking Patterns* 24
Chapter Eight: *The Path for Ordinary Practitioners: Levels of Understanding* 27
Chapter Nine: *Noble Ways of Thinking* 31
Chapter Ten: *Happiness* 36
Chapter Eleven: *Free of self-view* 38
Chapter Twelve: *Assumptions & Freedom from Bothersome Thoughts* 42
Chapter Thirteen: *The Middle Way & Nibbana* 50
-Theragāthā, Arahant Mahācunda 52
Chapter Fourteen: *Developing the Right View* 53
Chapter Fifteen: *Practical Middle Way* 56
Chapter Sixteen: *Understanding Conventions* 60
Chapter Seventeen: *Living Without Touching the Earth* ... 66
Chapter Eighteen: *The Direct Practice: Stream Entry* 69
Concluding Remarks 72
References 78

Preface

At this moment, there are several people around the world who are in need of healing and seeking ways to gain satisfaction in life. They may ask or they may not ask others, they may look like they are in distress, or they may not look like they are in distress, but they are most likely to be aware that their lives could be better if they knew how to resolve their unhelpful and bothersome thoughts.

This book discusses how one can develop knowledge of one's thoughts and self-help in overcoming discomforting thoughts. The guidance given here is based on the "middle way", an understanding of practical life according to Buddha's teachings. The teachings of the Buddha show us how to live life with satisfaction. Satisfaction can be gained in a mind by understanding one's thought process. This book discusses how you gain a balanced state of mind while going and doing your usual activities.

Chapter One:

The Journey to the Middle Way

Today's world is full of competition, people can feel overwhelming and stressful for many reasons. Rapid technological advancements, social and political issues, economic pressures, environmental concerns, work, money, and relationship-related issues including friends, and family-related matters, and various kinds of pressures can all contribute to a sense of unease. When worries pile up, your daily life experience can become unpleasant.

Maybe you find that your life is too joyful, or you fear that joys you enjoy will vanish too soon and wonder how long you can retain worldly joys. Maybe you find that your life is too painful, or you question whether you can handle it all. There may be parts of life that may be out of control and are difficult experiences for you. By understanding your painful thoughts, by understanding how thoughts come and go, and how pain is created, you can learn to reframe your thoughts through middle way practice to maintain a balanced mind and to make the most of your life while going and doing usual activities.

Beginning in childhood, it seems that almost everyone learns to do certain things well; how to eat well enough to prevent hunger; how to dress well enough to protect against environmental conditions;

and how to make a living to support continuation of physical body and life. But we don't learn how to learn and understand how to think well enough to reduce mental pain. Understanding how to think well enough within daily life can help you to reduce mental pain and extend worldly happiness.

Chapter Two:

Stream of Thoughts

Thoughts can behave like an ongoing stream just below your understanding, and, by understanding your thoughts, you can make gradual changes that will help you to think better and, in turn, pave your way to gaining peace and freedom from an ongoing stream of thoughts; a way of stream winning. When thinking in the best ways, middle way practice can allow you to retain worldly happiness.

Sometimes thoughts can bring happiness, sometimes unhappiness. Sometimes thoughts are generated based on what is happening in the external world. Sometimes thoughts happen on their own. Thoughts may wonder in a made-up past, a made-up present, or a made-up future, and so on. When someone tries to hold onto made-up things in thoughts, since made-up things are not the truth, they don't last, and they change. For example, when a "self" is made up, others and the world in thoughts, as they change, can bring distress and dissatisfaction in the mind. Similarly, grasping a made-up self, society and the world, and things that are happening to form, including illness and similar things, can generate thoughts such as happiness, unhappiness, gains, losses, and similar things, and, if one will continue to grasp a made-up self, the world and society can bring a lot of distress and dissatisfaction specially when things are changing. Events happen that are beyond our control, such as birth, death, illnesses, losses and similar things, and clinging to things that are not controllable makes little sense. Things that are not under our control can bring suffering, and, by understanding how much harm one's thoughts can do to oneself, a wise person will reflect wisely and not grasp one's thoughts and self that are made in thoughts, society and similar things but simply be functional; do what is best for oneself and others without too much holding on to one's thoughts or grasping but be free of such things.

The middle way is a practice of thinking that allows us to live in a world of imperfections without touching things in our minds. Middle-way thinking differs from common ways of thinking.

Thinking not in alignment with true life experience can make you develop a deluded thinking pattern that causes you mental pain. Understanding that change is the nature for all of us, without getting too worried over things that we cannot control or change, letting go of things that are gone, taking a reasonable course of action to do things that must be done, engaging to resolve things that can be resolved, and making the most of what is available, living life to the fullest is a wise thing to do. That is what middle mind training is about.

You may take all of your thoughts as an accurate reflection of truth or reality. Assuming if your taught were truly an accurate reflection of reality, it would be reasonable to assume that you would have no difficulty in accepting your life experiences as they come as what life becomes accepting your thoughts. Accepting whatever life experience without a regret is an awakening to truth, true life experience. Yet, when there is a discrepancy between what a person is thinking and what the person is experiencing on earth and in a person's life, a person can feel stress and inadequacy.

Thus, awakening to true; enlightenment means understanding how common ways of thinking produce mental pain to a greater extent. Understanding how mental pain is established in your mind will help you to escape such mental pain. Although it may seem easier to stay in the fantasy space where you would like to think that things you expect can be gained and all that you like can be fulfilled, understanding the differences between things that can be done and things that cannot be done will produce more benefit to you. Similarly, although it may be uncomfortable to think about giving up thinking patterns that have formed your "common ways of thinking", it may be even more uncomfortable for you to think about continuing them and continue to experience mental pain.

Chapter Three:

Ordinary Ways of Thinking

Ordinary ways of thinking, and societies that are created based on ordinary standards and to develop noble thinking, the practice requires training the mind to understand beyond ordinary ways "against the current ways of thinking and doing" (patisotagamini).

Common ways of thinking include getting attached to worldly experiences. Touching worldly experiences too much in mind is a common way, as is the inability to be satisfied with whatever way one presently has and instead seeking more and more worldly experiences. Thinking that it is possible to retain stability in self and worldly experiences, a person may develop a habit of touching worldly experiences too much in mind since birth. Thinking that the things on earth belong to a person, a person may grasp at changing worldly experiences. In this manner, what you think may not align with your true-life experiences.

Grasping at changing experiences is a common way of thinking since birth. Common ways of thinking are founded in social practices. Social practices based on standard ways of thinking teach people to think and behave in certain ways. Based on social learning and conditioning, people learn to associate happiness with winning and sadness with loosing, happiness at birth, and sadness at death. In this manner, since birth, people learn to connect certain things such as winning, gains, birth and the feelings of happiness that cause you to become happy. Similarly, people learn to connect certain things such as loosing, death and the feeling of sadness that cause you to become unhappy based on social learning and conditioning to interpret worldly experiences based on standard ways. Eventually, an association between events and responses is learned. You'll find that many, if not most, of your ways of thinking and actions can be traced back to standard ways of thinking and doing things.

Everything that a person thinks belongs to self can only fall short in worldly experiences. Based on sensory information and conventions, you tend to interpret self and the world in a limited way, which may not necessarily represent your true-life experience. For example, interpreting yourself as always gaining things or as not always gaining things as the way you would like to gain things are extreme ways of understanding life experience. Instead of making assumptions regarding what is possible to gain and what is not possible to gain and getting distressed when what is constructed in mind is not what is happening in life, a balanced mind can be maintained by understanding that there is no reason to be so worried over things that you lose, as loosing things is a part of life, both losses and gains are parts of life, both experiences subject to change. You can learn to develop a deeper understanding of life to maintain a balanced mind with wisdom to face events within daily life.

Identity views and social divisions are socially created constructs. What is socially constructed is subject to change. The underlying tendency you have for interpreting yourself as someone who should not face problems in life is deluded understanding. It's like wearing a pair of sunglasses. Understanding and accepting yourself as someone who should not experience problems can make you feel too upset when upsetting things happen in real life. In this manner, the screening of information coming through sense organs is processed based on how you understand and interpret things, which is how you make sense of you, others and the world and experience worldly life.

Understanding self as someone who can retain worldly experiences with stability can make you feel too upset when self and the experiences change following illnesses and changes in friendships and relationships and situations.

Interpreting someone as your friend and another person as not a friend can bring stress to you when a friend acts in a way that is opposed to what you interpreted. In this manner, how you understand and interpret self, others, situations, and worldly experiences will lead to your thoughts related to feelings and what you say and how you behave in situations.

The root cause of mental pain is how you interpret yourself and the situation based on too much greed you have for your thoughts, hatred you have in thoughts and your lack of (deluded) understanding the truth in your thoughts. Instead, by understanding how your thoughts work, you can take a step to free yourself from your mind when it brings too much mental pain to you. By applying wisdom, you can learn to make the most of your experiences.

The world is created in one's thoughts. When too many thoughts occupy one's mind, one may experience tiredness and weariness. Following standards that are established within societies, and ordinary ways, the vast majority of individuals in the world have a tendency in their minds to get attached to their thoughts.

Chapter Four:

Understanding Emptiness

Common ways of thinking are grasping at changing worldly experiences, and grasping refers to giving too much value to worldly experiences including social identities and social divisions in mind; dividing identities (I am young, I am old, I am rich, I am poor, I am a monk, I am a householder, etc.), dividing earth (I am from, my town is, etc.), dividing Dhamma (tradition, division, lifestyle, etc.) and similar ways. Although giving up social identities in worldly life is not practical, giving up clinging to such identities in mind is practical. Understand that clinging to social identities can produce mental pain. In this manner, middle-way training is a way of thinking that can be developed based on true life experience, so that one can learn to reframe thoughts to remain unaffected by self-view, social identities, and standard ways of thinking.

Grasping at changing worldly experiences produces mental pain. For example, for someone who thinks that there is stability in self, the uncertainty you are experiencing, and issues related to instability in self can bring mental pain. Uncertainty about the future can be in your thoughts, and you think "What if I have health issues that I don't know about?" or "What if I don't get a job" or "What if coronavirus rears its head again?". Suddenly, you may feel very uneasy. One way you could reduce feeling distress based on uncertainty is to develop a deeper understanding of life and focus your attention on resolving things around the situation instead of too much worrying about it; for example, you could remind yourself that uncertainty is a part of life. You might say to yourself "Uncertainty is a part of life, that's how life is, I need to figure out some ways to resolve things and let go of things that are gone at the same time, it's important that I make the most of present moment; I am ok, I've got a warm drink, and I've got things I need right now." In this manner, by understanding uncertainty is a part of life, by showing yourself compassion in difficult situations as that is what benefits you to reduce mental pain, telling yourself It's ok to feel uncomfortable about uncertainty but what is better is to think of how to resolve things instead of getting overly distressed about the situation, applying wisdom, you can let go of self-view and reduce mental pain.

For someone who thinks there is a stable self-based on social identities (age, lifestyle, etc.), social roles (father, monk, etc.), and divisions (country, tradition, etc.), instabilities and uncertainties related to views (identities, roles, and divisions) bring mental pain. For example, for someone who takes a parenting role can produce extreme stress when faced to meet with changing parenting experiences from time to time. For someone who takes a political role can produce extreme stress when faced to meet with changing experiences relevant to the role from time to time. It might sound obvious, but the ups and downs of life are just part of life.

Understanding the truth is that life will always have ups and downs will help you soften the lows and reduce mental pain.

Is the eye permanent or impermanent?" "Impermanent, sir." "But if it's impermanent, is it suffering or happiness?" "Suffering, sir." "But if it's impermanent, suffering, and perishable, is it fit to be regarded thus: 'This is mine, I am this, this is my self'?" "No, sir."

"Seeing this, a wise noble person becomes disillusioned with the eye, the ear, the nose, the tongue, the body, and the mind. Being disillusioned they become dispassionate. Being dispassionate they're freed. When freed, they know 'it is freed'. They understand: 'Rebirth is ended, the spiritual journey has been completed, what had to be done has been done, there is no return to any state of existence."
-SN 18.1, Cakkhusutta

The world's pretty things and pleasures are not the fetters, but the desire to experience or not experience such things is what causes mental pain. Experience things as they come without desiring excessively to experience or not experience certain things, without touching experiences too deep in the heart. Instead, remain unaffected by experiences and events by understanding they are a flow of events, and that uncertainty is a way of life. Understand that a person can escape grasping uncertainty to experience equanimity and a balanced mind in each moment.

"The eye is not the fetter of sights, nor are sights the fetter of the eye. The fetter there is the desire and greed that arises from the pair of them. The ear ... nose ... tongue ... body ... mind is not the fetter

of ideas, nor are ideas the fetter of the mind. The fetter there is the desire and greed that arises from the pair of them."
-SN 35.232, Koṭṭhikasutta

"What are the six kinds of lay equanimity? When seeing a sight with the eye, equanimity arises for the unlearned ordinary person—not applying wisdom, an ordinary person who has not overcome their limitations and the results of deeds, and is blind to the drawbacks. Such equanimity does not transcend the sight. That's why it's called lay equanimity. When hearing a sound with the ear ... When smelling an odor with the nose ... When tasting a flavor with the tongue ... When feeling a touch with the body ... When knowing an idea with the mind, equanimity arises for the unlearned ordinary person—an unwise ordinary person who has not overcome their limitations and the results of deeds, and is blind to the drawbacks. Such equanimity does not transcend the idea. That's why it's called lay equanimity. These are the six kinds of lay equanimity.

And in this context what are the six kinds of renunciate equanimity? When you've understood the impermanence of sights— their perishing, fading away, and cessation—equanimity arises as you truly understand through right understanding that both formerly and now all those sights are impermanent, suffering, and perishable. Such equanimity transcends the sight. That's why it's called renunciate equanimity. When you've understood the impermanence of sounds ... smells ... tastes ... touches ... ideas— their perishing, fading away, and cessation—equanimity arises as you truly understand through right understanding that both formerly and now all those ideas are impermanent, suffering, and perishable. Such equanimity transcends the idea. That's why it's called renunciate equanimity. These are the six kinds of renunciate equanimity".

-MN137, Saḷāyatanavibhaṅgasutta

Without interpreting things based on conventions, thoughts can be empty. For example, if somebody were to wake you up from a deep sleep and say that someone called John is waiting for you at the door, before kind of making sense of who John is, you are likely to experience a few empty thoughts.

To get to an empty state in your thoughts, you have to learn to let go of clinging to the fetters in daily life. Nibbana is about letting go in phases; first three fetters are self-view, social practices and conventions, and doubt. Giving up fetter refers to giving up desires in a middle way and giving up desires refers to giving up too many expectations, likes, and dislikes towards worldly experiences in a middle way within daily life.

The middle path is to be applied to let go of fetters in phases:

"When you know the Dhamma to be similar to a raft, you should abandon even the teachings, how much more so things contrary to the teachings."
-MN 22-Alagaddupama Sutta

"Together with his attainment of insight, three qualities have been abandoned (by him), namely: self-view, doubt and dependence on social practices (conventions, rituals and ceremonies)"

-Snp 2.1-Ratana Sutta

People are born with sense organs (eyes, ears, nose, tongue, and skin) that are open to receive sensory experiences from the external world. Sense organs have limitations. For example, eyes have limited frequency response and can see light only at limited wavelengths, and ears can hear sounds only at certain frequencies. Similarly, people interpret self, others and the world based on conventions, and conventions are limited ways of understanding self, others and the world. Social identities, divisions, language, concepts, and traditions are some of the examples of conventions, common ways upon which people across societies agree.

Since birth, people construct self-view (others and the world) based on conventions; age, class, nationality, lifestyle, and gender are socially constructed identities, and grasping at such conventions refers to things that are commonly accepted and practiced among people across societies. By understanding that self-view is strengthened by social practices, that certain ways of doing things in societies can divide people, and that certain social practices can put pressure on people and affect their wellbeing, one with wisdom will likely want to but be free from the need to give too much value to social practices (rituals and life styles) and instead become a good person true to one's own heart and do good to others by fulfilling responsibilities without expecting anything from others. This can produce inner satisfaction and mental peace. For example, standard ways of doing things and social practices make it a norm to become sad when losing things and become happy when gaining things. Similarly, it seems that society can sometimes portray that one can have a perfect life, perfect relationship, perfect household, perfect school grades, and a perfect job and similar ways. Yet, in real life, it is not always possible to have perfect things, and this is something one gets to learn from one's own life experience, a realization. When the real-life experiences fail to meet what one expects to experience in one's mind, one can feel disappointed. Therefore, by understanding that grasping earthly things too much can bring stress to oneself, a wise person will likely want to let go of clinging to earthly experiences including social practices and rituals.

Understanding true life experience and how your thoughts function and applying wisdom to reframe our thoughts to reduce mental pain is practicing the middle way in daily life. Worrying excessively over things that cannot be changed (certain downfalls of life, death, separations, illness, losses already happened) are not wise. Understand with wisdom that worrying alone doesn't help resolve situations, and mental pain is difficult to bear and not worth the pain. Instead, stop clinging to worrying experiences in your mind, a wise application of the middle way in daily life. It does not require you to maintain a posture like when engaging in ordinary meditation practices. The middle way practice can be practiced even when you are severely ill or are undergoing difficult situations.

Chapter Five:

Life Experiences

Understanding how to deal with daily life experiences is what will help you face with true life experiences. All sorts of distress; severe sadness, disappointment, fear, and anxiety come to your mind when what you expect to happen doesn't happen or will not happen based on assumptions and uncertainty surrounding your expectations. Too many expectations come because of your excessive likes and dislikes towards worldly experiences, which is a universally applicable truth. In this manner, a whole circle of mental suffering, whether it's called sadness or loss, establishes in someone's mind, because they are clinging to earth and seeking too much to touch the world in their mind. Expecting too much from things that you do and expecting too much from others can cause too much mental pain when things and others do not meet your expectations. The way that is not helpful is expecting what you expect should happen, as there is no guarantee that what you think can always happen. Instead, both what you expect and don't expect can happen; uncertainty is a part of life. Therefore, reflecting the truth that is applicable in life, maintaining a balanced mind is a wise application of the middle way in daily life.

What is universally applicable truth is that people do not have the full ability to control every situation, and experience on earth. If you can understand that change is in nature and ups and downs of life are part of everyone's life; and maintain that understanding throughout your day and night; let go of things that are gone; make the most of life; attend to tasks that need attending to without expecting that the tasks will or will not bring out expected results, but simply puts one's best efforts. Doing these things will allow you to resolve issues in the best possible way while keeping worries down. Cultivating your wisdom, so that you know the difference between what you can and can't change, and doing what you can do to resolve things, let go of things that are not possible to change a wise approach to life.

Chapter Six:

Awakening

Nature makes everyone face all kinds of experiences in life. The thoughts that pass through a person's mind make a view of self, others, and the world. Yet, it may happen that a natural autonomous thinking process for the untrained mind of an ordinary person will cause the person more likely to think and expect that life can be filled only with good things when they try to make sense of the world coming through sensory experience. In doing so, the person may interpret either consciously or unconsciously that what is made up in the mind is more important than what is experienced in real life. The person may allocate more attention to what is made up in the mind. Thinking in that manner, an ordinary person is likely to expect and more willing to accept only the good things in life. For example, in general, people find that birth is an easy concept to process (birth is more accepted) and that death is a difficult concept to process (less accepted or accepted unwillingly to a greater extent); good health is more accepted, and bad health is less accepted; laughter is more accepted, and crying is less accepted. In this manner, people tend to make a list of what is accepted and what is not accepted in their minds. When an ordinary person continues to process information coming from sensory organs based on what the person is thinking and making up in the mind as real as opposed to what the person is experiencing in real life, such thoughts, which are bias, can lead to delusion.

Although real life experience will show that both ups and downs are part of life for people, mind-made understanding of a person's world can be different from that of real-life experience. When there is a discrepancy between what is real and what is made up in one's mind, the difference between real life experience and a person's mind-made understanding of the person's world can create an ongoing tension and stress to the person when they mismatch, and harmony and peace can be lost in the person's mind. By bringing mind-made understanding of the person's world closer to real-life experience, the person will be able to gain harmony to restore satisfaction gained through worldly life.

When faced with unpleasant events, an ordinary person is likely to suffer too much distress, particularly when the person's mind is in the habit of hiding certain aspects of life if they are not a part of life. Instead, stop hiding things that are a part of life to see with clarity by allowing the mind to understand and interpret real life experience to understand that ups and downs are natural for all of us. In doing so, let go of cognitive bias that results in clinging to mind-made things as if they are real. A wise person can develop an understanding to see beyond ordinary views. Having a limited and restricted understanding of life can produce too much stress. Instead, by reducing thinking erroneously with bias and becoming free from a limited understanding of life and the mind, a person can develop the right understanding of life and mind. The right view/correct understanding of life will allow a person to extend happiness gained through worldly experience (cutting off worldly experiences by cutting off sensory experiences is not practical, as worldly experiences are processed through sensory information in each person) while living with conventions.

Once born, a person comes to experience changes that are brought on by nature. Caught between nature in the universe and worldly experience coming from sensory information, a person may develop a self, others, and the world in the person's thoughts. While living on earth, a person may think certain things, and what a person is thinking may not happen in real life. When there is a discrepancy between what a person is thinking and what the person is experiencing on earth and in a person's life, a person can feel stress and inadequacy.

Not understanding the truth can produce mental pain. Understanding truth allows a person to experience worldly life without regret. Understanding that change is the nature for all of us, instead of just watching how things unfold, and without getting too worried over things that we cannot control or change, letting go of things that are gone, taking a reasonable course of action to do things that must be done, engaging to resolve things that can be resolved, and making the most of what is available, living life to the fullest is a wise thing to do. When a person understands with wisdom that certain things in the universe cannot be changed, that not everything can be gained, and that the person should therefore let go of things that cannot be changed but attend to doing the things that can be done without regret, this is a wise thing to do; it is a way of developing the middle mind training to abandoning self-view and to achieving the noble way of living. Instead of too much dependence on others and on society for approval or denial and expecting from others and society, a person chooses to do good and avoid doing bad and is true to one's heart, one can find inner peace within despite what other people think and say. In this manner, a person can remain satisfied and unaffected in the very presence of others and the world, not hurting oneself and not hurting others, and that is a way of developing the middle path.

Chapter Seven:

Thinking Patterns

Since birth, people are trained to think in a structured framed way. Standard ways of thinking encourage people to touch worldly life too much in their minds and to maintain a restricted vision by getting stuck into man-made identities, divisions, systems (political, economic systems, ways of having a birthday party, graduating, becoming a monk based on rituals, conducting a funeral), and ways of doing things and conventions (language, words, etc.) including the common ordinary ways of thinking.

Based on standard ways of thinking, a child may be encouraged to think: "I can become happy when I will become an adult and have a career"; a young adult may be encouraged to think: "I can become happy when I will finish my degree"; and an older person may think: "I can become happy when I retire", all based on ordinary ways of thinking. From childhood, people are told to seek satisfaction in things that they do not have and to think of things they should gain in times that are yet to come. In this manner, ordinary standards encourage us to live in times in which we do not live and expect things we do not have. We are encouraged to cling into the worldly experiences again and again; it goes as a thinking cycle. Based on ordinary ways, since birth, everyone gets stuck in a system of thinking that tricks them into a cycle of pain and binds them again and again.

Similarly, one of the common ordinary ways of thinking includes seeking satisfaction through worldly experiences and setting targets with an attached mind state in an endless manner. For example, a child is encouraged to work toward finishing school, an adult is encouraged to get a job or career and an older person is encouraged to retire consisting of slowing activities down and ultimately death. Having such goals is one thing but thinking that the goals are going to retain with stability and with an underlying tendency to get too attached to them in one's mind. liking, disliking or expecting too much out of such goals and worldly experiences is another thing. A mind that grasps goals too much or touches the goals too much in the mind (with greediness, hatred or delusion) can cause a person to experience mental suffering. Thus, having goals and working for them is not the root cause of mental sufferings; the root cause is the mind that has too many expectations and too many likes and dislikes toward worldly life. An untrained mind can struggle to find happiness and satisfaction in worldly experiences. Yet, if you understand that it is meaningless to experience mental pain over things that are inevitably changing, you can train and reframe your thoughts to experience happiness in each new moment irrespective of circumstances.

Since birth, everyone follows a common way of thinking. Yet, at some point or over time, some people realize that they experience mental pain or mental pressure in their lives when trying to keep up with common ways of thinking and doing. When people understand it with wisdom, they can escape the cycle of thinking.

In this manner, by understanding Buddha's Dhamma, you can cross the ordinary ways of thinking through middle way. Based on your life experiences, if you understand that conventions and worldly experiences are subject to change, this realization is the first step toward understanding. Then, if you understand that things that begin come to end in worldly life, that is in the natural and universal functioning of all beings. Therefore, you will realize that clinging to changing things leads to experiencing mental pain, which is hard to endure and not worthwhile. This realization is the second step of understanding. Given that things are changing anyway within worldly life, letting go of grasping changing experiences is a wise thing for the wellbeing of yourself and others (so that you can become a happier person, and happier people can share happiness with others). This is the third step of understanding. These three steps can help you develop middle mind training.

By understanding your personal experience with wisdom, the realization of life experiences, and truth, you can learn to reframe your thinking to accept the truth that is applicable to all; let go of things that are gone (do not grasp them too much in your mind creating stress), focus and attend to things that need attention, look after yourself and others to the best level while they are there. Wisdom is required to think beyond standard ways of thinking.

Chapter Eight:

The Path for Ordinary Practitioners: Levels of Understanding

Based on personal experience, a person can gain a deeper understanding of real life and awaken to true life experiences that are universally applicable for all. Gaining a deeper understanding of real-life experiences is different from simply accepting something or a belief or faith. This is because belief indicates likelihood of acceptance; accepting something as likely with a degree of certainty indicates a lower level of understanding on a continuum of understanding the path leading to Nibbana. In this manner, the path leading to Nibbana has various levels of understanding. Instead, when the belief that real life experiences or that worldly life is painful becomes a certainty - when an ordinary person understands that worldly life experiences are surely painful without a doubt, that is their entry point to the middle way practice.

Thinking that happiness and joy gained out of worldly experiences can last forever, an ordinary person touches the world in mind since birth, liking and disliking worldly experiences too much again and again. As joy and pleasures arise from worldly experiences, liking them too much, a person may expect to experience more and more joys and pleasures through worldly life. Yet, changes happen to joys and pleasures experienced through worldly life; joys can turn into sorrow, and pleasures can turn in to displeasures. Often, it is the same thing you liked the most that produce the most mental pain when it changes. In this manner, based on common ways of thinking, an ordinary person (since birth everyone walks in this path) may initially be baffled and experience disbelief or shock when forced to experience changing worldly experiences in life. Life experience can vary from trauma to relationship issues, to financial struggles, to illnesses, to the death of a close associate and various other difficult worldly experiences including social economic pressures. Yet, based on personal life experiences, if a person comes to understand without a doubt that worldly life and common ways of think indeed bring mental pain, thus grasping changes is meaningless, because they are going to change anyway. Instead, making the most of them is a wise thing to do. In this manner, awakening to truth means understanding life experiences with wisdom to a greater extent.

If an ordinary person has doubts regarding worldly life, the person may think that worldly life can produce more joys, and the person is unlikely to want to give up clinging to worldly experiences in the minds despite the person's lifestyle and meditation practices. Instead, those who feel that their whole world has collapsed, and all dreams have crashed, if they are wise, they are more likely to have the ability to remove doubts about worldly life experience to gain a realization that their clinging to worldly life brings mental suffering to them.

Experiencing as if the world has collapsed on them and crashing the world as experienced by each person in one's own thoughts is a subjective process, as it depends on how each person interprets and makes sense of the extent to which their world is collapsing, and their dreams are shattering in their thoughts. However, given that realization is a subjective process and subject to one's wisdom, it is possible that a person will realize that clinging to worldly life can produce sufferings by experiencing just one or two bad incidents and events in the person's life. For another person, it can take a little longer to understand. For example, a person may realize that clinging to worldly life can produce suffering by experiencing several bad incidents and events in one's life. In any case, a wise person will eventually come to understand and realise through life experience that clinging to worldly life can produce suffering through personal experience. For them, it would make sense to give up clinging to worldly experiences, to let go of unbearable suffering, to experience stable peace and to enhance worldly satisfaction gained through sensory information through Middle path within their daily life. In this manner, middle path is very practical.

Based on one's personal life experiences, if someone endures various kinds of worldly hardships and understands for themselves that life is not easy, that is the kind of an understanding that helps an ordinary practitioner want to practice middle mind training. At the next level, if an ordinary person understands that grasping worldly life can without a doubt produce mental pain, and it's not worth the pain, that kind of understanding helps an ordinary practitioner to continue training in the middle path. Otherwise, one may just hear and talk about the path and live a lifestyle without necessarily applying the middle path training. Thus, practicing Dhamma for an ordinary practitioner means applying Dhamma to oneself, and, as the result of applying Dhamma practice, should reduce one's pride, greediness, and extreme sadness towards worldly experiences. If these things are not reduced, it is unreasonable to say that one has practiced Dhamma despite one's years in meditation practice.

Chapter Nine:

Noble Ways of Thinking

Identities are formed during childhood, and, with them, people build up expectations of other people and of things around based on their formulated identities. For example, a child learns to identify self and to develop the expectation of receiving care from parents based on the understanding that a child can receive care from parents, friendship from friends, and lack of friendship from those who are not friends. When a person develops likes and dislikes towards what one experiences as self, others and the world in one's mind, and when likes and dislikes are mismatched, and when a person's expectations do not meet their experience from self, others and the world as experienced in one's thoughts, a person can experience stress.

The universe functions in such a manner that people are faced with the ups and downs of life. Ordinary practitioners can develop middle way training by applying the understanding of how the universe functions, the understanding that ups and downs are part of life for everyone, by doing things that are needed and beneficial without too much worrying, by reducing expectations as a way of following Buddha's Dhamma, and by walking towards the noble path. This is what is referred to as middle-mind training. Social practices (rituals) further strengthen the self-view, others and the world and train to gain Nibbana, which means giving up clinging, avoiding giving too much value to social practices in one's mind and such thoughts rather becoming a good person doing good, and avoiding bad things by being true to one's heart. In this manner, a person can develop a self-practice, responsibility and independence to be free from clinging to self-view, others, and a worldly life. Given that the self-view and the worldly life are experienced by all people in their thoughts and not out of their own thoughts, Buddha's path shows how a person can find satisfaction and gain freedom from self-view and others in their thoughts. The self knows the best about the self. For example, a person who puts all efforts in doing good and avoiding bad can be free from self-blaming, blaming others and the world. For example, a person who is very sick will attempt to get treatment for the sickness to the best of the person's capacity, while maintaining reduced expectations. This will allow the person to find satisfaction and the best possible way to resolve the problem at the same time. Therefore, wisdom to apply middle-mind training and thinking beyond ordinary ways and ability to apply Dhamma to oneself are preliminary qualifications that will allow one to find satisfaction, peace, and cease to exist in mind; Nibbana.

Thinking that it is possible to retain stability in self and worldly experiences, a person may develop a habit of touching the worldly experiences too much in mind since birth. You may take common ways of thinking as an accurate reflection of truth or reality. Yet, when changes happen in self and worldly experiences, the way you are thinking based on common ways may not match the true-life experiences. When the things that happen in life don't align with what you are thinking, and when what you were expecting to experience is not what is happening in life, you can feel dissatisfaction.

The ordinary way of thinking is what is common, what is common is what is socially created, what is socially created does not align with things that happen in a person's life based on universal ways; birth, death, illnesses and ups and downs that everyone experiences in worldly life. What is socially constructed (views; stable self, others and the world including conventions) is not given a value or importance by the universe and its way of functioning. All beings regardless of their social identities and divisions must experience birth, death, ups and downs at random times. Thus, common ways of thinking that are socially created have limitations; such thinking does not align with a person's true-life experiences.

"An ordinary person who has not gained Nibbana, who has no understanding about the noble ones, and is not skilled and not disciplined in their Dhamma practice, who has no regard for true disciples of the Buddha and is unskilled and undisciplined in their Dhamma, does not understand what things are fit for attention and what things are unfit for attention. Since that is so, one attends to those things unfit for attention and one does not attend to those things fit for attention.."

"This is how one attends unwisely: 'Was I in the past? Was I not in the past? What was I in the past? How was I in the past? Having been what, what did I become in the past? Shall I be in the future? Shall I not be in the future? What shall I be in the future? How shall I be in the future? Having been what, what shall I become in the future?' Or else he is inwardly perplexed about the present thus: 'Am

I? Am I not? What am I? How am I? Where has this being come from? Where will it go?'
-MN2, Sabbāsavasutta

Thus, truth that it is universally applicable for everyone is that whatever they have is subject to change and that, when changes happen to worldly experiences, certain changes can bring mental sufferings.

"The Dhamma is not a convention; speculative philosophy, but is the universal happening gained through four-fold Nibbana and is preached precisely"
-AN 11.12

It is universally applicable is that mental pain can be reduced by understanding true life experiences; life has both ups and downs and natural and universal functioning. Mental pain can be reduced by reducing mental attachment to changing worldly experiences within daily life.

The noble way of thinking is not grasping identities that are socially created in mind, because it is meaningless to cling to identities that are changing anyway. Identity views (I am young, I am old, I am a monk, I am a singer) and social divisions are socially created constructs. What is socially constructed is subject to change.

Noble ways of thinking do not divide the earth by grasping (meaning not giving too much value to such things in mind; I am from this country ... I am better...) and grasping to self-view in many ways.

For someone who thinks that there is no stability in self (self-view), instability in self is unlikely to bring too much mental pain.

To practice noble way of thinking, you have to surpass the majority way of thinking and doing. For example, let's say that in a particular region, the majority of individuals engage in killing living beings, or treating others differently based on conventions (gender, class, nationality, age, education, position) and, for them that is a normal thing to do as accepted within social practices. Instead, a person who aspires inner peace through middle way practice will decide for oneself that, just because others engage in killing living beings or engage in things that are causing distress to others (e.g. Differential treatment towards others), that person does not need to be engaged in doing such things. This allows a practitioner to develop self-responsibility, a self-practice to do good irrespective of what others are doing and saying.

In this manner, despite others physical presence (or absence), if you choose to do always good, you can find peace within. When you surpass the majority way or common way of thinking and doing, you can find peace and satiation within that is hard to find in common ways.

Chapter Ten:

Happiness

The middle-way practice can be gained by reducing the likes, dislikes, and expectations within one's lifestyle and daily life. This is because one can experience self, others and the world only as a subjective experience. Even the mind that discriminates between subject and object is still a subjective experience. In other words, given that a person can experience self only within one's thoughts and not within another person's thoughts and the mind, the practice of letting go likes and dislikes and expectations in the middle-way remains a subjective experience of letting go of one's self-view, others, and the world.

The middle-way is a practice that subject to a person; it does not require changing one's life style but reducing likes, dislikes, and expectations within one's life style and daily life. This explains why practitioners who are living in monastic settings and in non-monastic settings, practitioners of any tradition and even those who practice no spiritual practice, can reduce their liking, disliking and expectations for worldly experiences that are coming from sensory experiences within their lifestyles when they make their life style supportive to them in a way that will practice the middle-way in their minds. In their thoughts, they will be able to reduce sufferings. For those who live in a monastic setting (based on social standards and rituals) may use their monastic lifestyle to support their practicing to give up likes, dislikes and expectations within their lifestyle. For them, their monastic life style will serve as their middle-way practicing within their thoughts.

For a king, renunciation refers to reducing likes, dislikes and expectations within thoughts while continuing to live the lifestyle of a king (from a conventional sense) without getting attached to the view of self, others and the world experiences that are coming from sensory experiences. Buddha's Dhamma can be practiced by anyone anywhere within their lifestyle, and the practice remains the same for all times.

Chapter Eleven:

Free of self-view

How can you be free of self-view?

You can reduce self-view by reducing liking and disliking towards daily experiences and events and thereby reduce desires towards experiencing certain things and not desiring to experiencing certain things within daily life. This is because the mere presence of material or physical things is not the reason for stress, which is instead caused by the desire to experience and the desire not to experience physical and material things.

Similarly, understand that interpreting based on common ways produces mental suffering for us. In doing so, try to reduce getting upset when faced with bad events and reduce the tendency of one's mind to become too happy when faced with good events by understanding that happiness can change. Instead, try not to separate experiences as good or bad, a technique one can use to train the mind slowly to maintain stable peace and be happy with whatever one possesses, which will help one gain contentment in daily life.

Similarly, understand that one person has no control of another person, which is not surprising as one does not even have a control of one's own mind. Understand that it is not always possible to control a mind, but it is possible to be free of a mind and therefore not expect anything from others but just to do things for the benefit of others without expectations. Not expecting anything in return will allow one to gain satisfaction and remain satisfied, which is a technique that one can use to abandon self-view.

Another technique to reduce self-view is to understand the uncertainty of life, change the nature of things, and not ignore the truth that is applicable to our lives. Gains, materials, life style, youth, relationships, and similar things don't last forever. One's body, mind, friends and family, relationships, gains, and similar things are subject to change. We must understand that change and uncertainty are part of life for all of us and make the most of every day and our lives by doing good things and abandoning unwholesome things, not becoming proud, not treating others differently due to their backgrounds, not using materials, knowledge or whatever one possesses for the benefit of self alone rather sharing with others in a kind and humble and gentle manner, fulfilling responsibilities towards others, becoming a good person and collecting merits. These actions can help practitioners gain Nibbana. Just as we jump up on earth, we fall back. The law of karma is applicable to all. Thus, for one who collects merits, the wisdom, materials, gains and Nibbana will follow through naturally due to the functioning of the universe.

Similarly, understand that an aspect of self-view is strengthened by one's attachment towards rituals, social groups, social divisions and societies. Societies are man-made, geographical locations, identities, and divisions. Rituals are man-made. Understanding that, at the end of life and at the death bed, we must give up all such things and to go into samsara unless one gains four-fold Nibbana, which comes as a result of one's karma, is a useful way of reflection for understanding Nibbana. Due to the diversity of karma, a person's background does not have an impact on Nibbana. Therefore, understanding that life is short, making the most of life by becoming content with whatever one possesses for now and doing good and trying to develop a higher understanding Dhamma will benefit those practitioners who aspire gaining Nibbana. One can abandon fetters (non-self-view, rites and rituals, precepts, doubts) by practicing in the middle way, may it be a text book, division, or the lifestyle of a monk, or lifestyle of a householder, saying "I have a lifestyle" or " I do not have a lifestyle" indicates two sides and the middle way training meaning, having or not having should be given equal value or importance, in doing so simply use what is available for improving wisdom and deep understanding of Dhamma, higher wisdom towards arahanthship and become a good person without clinging to such things. Clinging is not a helpful practice when such clinging give rise to identity views (for example, divisions that are socially created) and strengthens such views.

In sum, being free of self-view, of grasping or giving too much value to socially created identities (age, gender, location, lifestyle of a monk, etc.) that are created by following society's practices, and standards such as rituals, divisions, traditions, religion in one's mind, and being free of doubts are all needed to gain the Stream Entry stage. Doubts about Buddha can be removed by understanding that Buddha is the teacher of men and gods. Those who want to gain Nibbana should understand that Buddha became Buddha by completing training over many lives (Paramis), that Buddha is unique and cannot be replaced by another, that, similarly, the teachings of Buddha cannot be replaced by another person's teachings and that Nibbana and the teachings of Buddha can be understood by hearing Dhamma from Buddha and Arahants.

Chapter Twelve:

Assumptions & Freedom from Bothersome Thoughts

To a greater extent, subject to individual differences, the understanding of an ordinary person regarding Buddha's Dhamma remains at a conceptual level. For example, from a philosophical point of view, an ordinary practitioner may say that all dharmas have one nature, which is no-nature, because the ultimate nature of all phenomena is emptiness. In that case, those who apply the philosophy to themselves should give up worrying too much about the past, getting too anxious about the future, worrying too much about the present, treating others differently thinking one is better, worse or the same as others, give up pride, and similar things such as worrying over empty things would make no sense and being proud of things that are empty of self-would be meaningless. Similarly, from a philosophical point of view, if an ordinary practitioner says that being is made of five aggregates and sensory experiences, in that case those who apply such a philosophy to themselves should give up worrying too much about the past, getting too anxious about the future, worrying too much about the present, treating others differently thinking one is better, worse or the same as others, give up pride, and similar things such as worrying about experiences produced by five aggregates that are changing, this would be meaningless. Being proud of things that are changing would make no sense for a wise person. Things such as worrying too much about experiences produced by five aggregates would make no sense. Being proud of experiences produced by five aggregates as a being would be meaningless. This explains the gap between the conceptual understanding of Dhamma and the application of the concept into oneself.

> *"A person who associates oneself with certain views, considering them as best and making them supreme in the world, one says, because of that, that all other views are inferior; therefore, one is not free from contention (with others). In what is seen, heard, cognized and in ritual observances performed, one sees a profit for oneself. Just by laying hold of that view one regards every other view as worthless. Those skilled (in judgment) say that (a view becomes) a bond if, relying on it, one regards everything else as inferior. Therefore, a person should not depend on what is seen, heard or cognized, nor upon ritual observances. One should not present oneself as equal to, nor imagine himself to be inferior, nor better than, another".*
>
> SN 4.5, Paramatthaka Sutta

At times, the concept of "oneness" used by ordinary practitioners to describe Buddha's Dhamma suggest there is an interconnection between beings, hinting that there is a permanent being. Such concepts don't clarify Buddha's Dhamma in full, as Buddha's Dhamma refers to Sotapanna to Arahant. Similarly, if respect for all living things is an expression of oneness, then there are good people who respect all living things even without a spiritual practice, and they should all be able to gain Nibbana simply by developing compassion. However, compassion alone is not sufficient to gain Sotapanna.

What seems to be happening in the societies is that some of the common assumptions and practices based on such common assumptions have prevented Nibbana for those who understood and practiced in common ways. The path leading to Nibbana remains the same for all.

There are many assumptions, including traditions, because ordinary practitioners lack integrity; when they describe a path that they have not gained, they can mislead others.

> *"It's not the nature that make the true teaching disappear. Rather, it's the foolish people who appear among ordinary Sangha that make the true teaching disappear. The true teaching doesn't disappear like a ship that sinks all at once.*
>
> *There are five detrimental things that lead to the decline and disappearance of the true teaching. What five? It's when the ordinary bhikkhus (male, female), ordinary householders (male, female) lack respect and reverence for the Buddha, the Buddha's Dhamma (Sotapanna to Arahant), the noble Saṅgha (Sotapanna to Arahant), the practice leading to four-fold Nibbana, and immersion. These five detrimental things lead to the decline and disappearance of the true teaching.*
>
> *There are five things that lead to the continuation, persistence, and enduring of the true teaching. What five? It's when the ordinary bhikkhus (male, female), ordinary householders (male, female) lack respect and reverence for the Buddha, the Buddha's Dhamma (Sotapanna to Arahant), the noble Saṅgha (Sotapanna to Arahant), the practice leading to four-fold Nibbana, and immersion., and immersion. These five things lead to the continuation, persistence, and enduring of the true teaching."*
>
> -SN 16.13, Saddhammappatirūpakasutta

Middle Path (and Nibbana) is a universal remedy for mental pain experienced by people across the world and has nothing to do with any socially constructed religion, identities, divisions, or lifestyles. Dhamma (Sotapanna to Arahant) is universal. Ordinary practitioners seem to think and suggest that there are different ways to gain Nibbana for individuals from different backgrounds based on their assumptions. For example, one of the common assumptions is that individuals from different countries/traditions/lifestyles should follow different practices of Dhamma (e.g., Western and Eastern Buddhism). However, the middle-way practice including the path to Nibbana remains the same for all; abandoning the fetters and developing confirmed confidence in the Triple Gem.

Can a person let go of self-view by reading stories, engaging in academic studies, living a ritualistic life? No, none of these are ways to abandon self-view. This is because reading stories, engaging in academic studies, and maintaining a lifestyle based on rituals and maintaining sila alone (i.e., control over verbal and bodily actions with an underlying tendency to like and dislike worldly experiences) does not allow a person to purify thoughts from clinging to worldly experiences coming through sensory information.

"Though one recites much the Sacred Texts (Tipitaka) but is negligent and does not apply Dhamma to oneself (and does not practice) according to the Dhamma, like a cowherd who counts the cattle of others, one is unable to gain the benefits of Dhamma (i.e., Magga-phala)".

> *"Though one recites only a little of the Sacred Texts (Tipitaka), but practises according to the Dhamma, give up fetters, ill will and ignorance, clearly comprehending the four-fold Nibbana, possessing noble virtues and no longer clinging to this world or to the next, one gains the benefit of Dhamma (i.e., Magga-phala)".*
> -Dhp 19 & 20

Another assumption constructed by ordinary practitioners seems to suggest that Nibbana can be gained by developing mindfulness. In doing so, ordinary practitioners seem to ignore the key role played by merits, Buddha, and the noble order. Can a person let go of self-view by maintaining conscious awareness? No, and this is because Nibbana cannot be gained through the will of a person by maintaining conscious awareness that is subject to change.

Nibbana is a happening at a universal level, just as birth happens at random times at random locations to random families, and death, ups and downs are experiences that come to people at random times, Nibbana is an experience that comes to each person who purifies thoughts from clinging to worldly experiences to let go of self-view and develop confirmed confidence in Triple Gem at random times.

Not understanding Nibbana, you can come up with doubts, various assumptions and presumptions. Looking for reasoning can allow an ordinary practitioner to make sense of Nibbana. Without understanding the direct path and the practice, practitioners can be lost in their practices without gaining Nibbana, as, for centuries, Nibbana is rare.

In this manner, what you think is not what it is; Nibbana, Nibbana can be prevented for you.

To train to cessation, giving up in mind refers to giving up getting attached to one's thoughts that make up the presence of materials, the world, self-view, and others in one's mind. In other words, whatever material things are physically present and whatever the world is physically present should not interfere with one's mind.

Given that the practice of letting go is universally applicable, shaped by one's karma and merits, people with various backgrounds can gain Nibbana if they follow the direct path; giving up the fetters through the middle way while developing the confirmed confidence in the Triple Gem.

> *"Now at that time Sarakāni the Sakyan had passed away. The Buddha declared that he was a stream-enterer, not liable to be reborn in the underworld, bound for awakening.*
>
> *At that, several Sakyans (relatives of Buddha) came together complaining, grumbling, and objecting, "Oh, how incredible, how amazing! Who can't become a stream-enterer these days? For the Buddha even declared Sarakāni to be a stream-enterer after he passed away. Sarakāni was too weak for the training; he used to drink alcohol."*

> *Then Mahānāma the Sakyan went up to the Buddha, bowed, sat down to one side, and told him what had happened. The Buddha said:*
>
> *"Mahānāma, when a person truly follows and make a refuge for self by going to refuge in to the Buddha, Buddha' Dhamma, and the noble Saṅgha, how could they go to the underworld? And if anyone should rightly be said to have for a long time gone for refuge to the Buddha, the teaching, and the Saṅgha, it's Sarakāni the Sakyan. Sarakāni the Sakyan has for a long time gone for refuge to the Buddha, the teaching, and the Saṅgha."*
>
> -SN 55.2, Paṭhamasaraṇānisakkasutta

As illustrated in Sarakāni case, most of the ordinary people could not understand Nibbana even when they were in the presence of the Buddha.

People who have not yet gained Nibbana will struggle to understand Nibbana, as Nibbana cannot be compared to anything we would know in this world or what is commonly heard about.

Regarding the practice of abandoning the relevant fetters, you can train to abandon a non-self-view (rites, and rituals, and doubts) by training the mind in the middle way in daily life. For example, by understanding that life is impermanent and that ups and downs are part of life for all of us and are universally applicable to all beings, one can train the mind not to become disheartened when faced with bad events and, similarly, not to become overjoyed when experiencing good events, as they do not last long, and, in doing so, train the mind in the middle way in daily life (middle mind training is given up at the arahant state to lead to cessation; until then, middle mind training is useful).

To become a noble person rites and rituals, ceremonies, schools and traditions, external factors (gender, age, appearance, nationality etc.) are not relevant, but one's level of gaining a deeper understanding of the stages of Nibbana (or attainment of Nibbana) and the extent of abandoning greed, hate and delusion is what applies. Given that Nibbana happens naturally shaped by Karma and merits, anyone anywhere practicing the teachings in a right manner will be able to gain fruition.

Chapter Thirteen:

The Middle Way & Nibbana

Middle mind training is a key component of the practice leading to stream-entry, Nibbana. Middle mind training is about how you can develop your thinking and understanding and reframe your thoughts to understand self and the world beyond conventions. To a greater extent, middle mind training can be developed by understanding the life experience with wisdom.

The teachings beyond ordinary views of Dhamma are rare, and those who are genuinely seeking Nibbana will benefit if they will reflect wisely and understand the teachings beyond ordinary views with reasoning, and not without reasonings.

Important it is to understand is that Nibbana is a training in mind, and the reason is because the world is created in one's mind, and self-view and others are created in one's mind and in one's thoughts.

To train to cessation, giving up in mind refers to giving up getting attached to one's thoughts that make up the presence of materials, the world, self-view, and others in one's mind. This is because quitting an ordinary world and conventions are not practical and feasible, as wherever one goes, whether in the forest or in the town, given that the ordinary world we live in is filled with conventions, one only gets to live with conventions. Thus, Buddha's Dhamma (Sotapanna to Arahant) shows how a person can find inner satisfaction while living with conventions in an ordinary world by giving up clinging to such conventions in the person's mind. In other words, whatever material things that are physically present and whatever the world is physically present should not interfere with one's mind.

Standard ways of thinking encourage people to touch worldly life too much in their minds and to maintain a restricted vision by getting stuck into man-made identities, divisions, systems (political, economic systems), rituals (ways of having a birthday party, graduating, conducting a funeral, becoming a monk based on rituals), and ways of doing things and conventions (language, words, etc.) including the common ordinary ways of thinking. Conventions allow continuation, and Nibbana allows cessation or cease to exist from conventions in mind, way of renunciation based on Buddha's ways.

People are born on the earth. Ups and downs are a part of life; they are what nature brings to each person. This cannot be forgotten, and, if forgotten, it will constantly be reminded to a person by nature. Similarly, nature brings Sotapanna to those who put genuine efforts into purifying their own mind by clinging to worldly experience; Sotapanna happens in its own time, just as ups and downs in life happen to a person in their own time. Experiencing worldly pleasures and gaining spiritual happiness at the same time, a Sotapanna gets to experience the best in both worldly life and spiritual life at the same time. Just as ups and downs of life are personal experiences for each person, Buddha's Dhamma across four-stages is a personal experience for each person. Therefore, Buddha's Dhamma is not a concept, theory, meditation practice, division, tradition, or convention. Buddha's Dhamma is a happening just like birth for beings. Nibbana is a universal happening.

To practice middle mind training; understanding that there is no permanent self, uncertainty is a part of life, mental pain through changing worldly life experience is not worth; instead focusing on things that need attending without getting too much distress a wise thing to do; in doing so, train the mind to reduce attachment mentally in daily life. Along with middle mind training, if a person can develop factors of stream-entry by attending and reflecting the qualities of the Triple Gem, Nibbana will happen in its own time. The reason is Nibbana is a happening at universal level.

"The one who put an attempt to listen to the Buddha's Dhamma, knowledge of true Dhamma increases. A person can develop wisdom through that knowledge of Dhamma. Reality can be understood through that wisdom. Realizing the truth brings true happiness."

-Theragāthā, Arahant Mahācunda

Chapter Fourteen:

Developing the Right View

To a greater extent, subject to individual differences, the understanding of an ordinary person regarding Dhamma remains at a conceptual level. For example, from a philosophical point of view, an ordinary practitioner may say that all dharmas have one nature, which is no-nature, because the ultimate nature of all phenomena is emptiness. In that case, those who apply the philosophy to themselves should give up worrying too much about the past, getting too anxious about the future, worrying too much about the present, treating others differently thinking one is better, worse or the same as others, give up pride, and similar things such as worrying over empty things would make no sense and being proud of things that are empty of self-would be meaningless. Similarly, from a philosophical point of view, if an ordinary practitioner says that being is made of five aggregates and sensory experiences, in that case those who apply such a philosophy to themselves should give up worrying too much about the past, getting too anxious about the future, worrying too much about the present, treating others differently thinking one is better, worse or the same as others, give up pride, and similar things such as worrying about experiences produced by five aggregates that are changing, this would be meaningless. Being proud of things that are changing would make no sense for a wise person. Things such as worrying too much about experiences produced by five aggregates would make no sense. Being proud of experiences produced by five aggregates as a being would be meaningless. This explains the gap between the conceptual understanding of Dhamma and the application of the concept into oneself. At times, the concept of "oneness" used by ordinary practitioners to describe Buddha's Dhamma suggest there is an interconnection between beings, hinting that there is a permanent being. Such concepts don't clarify Buddha's Dhamma in full, as Buddha's dhamma refers to Sotapanna to Arahant. Similarly, if respect for all living things is an expression of oneness, then there are good people who respect all living things even without a spiritual practice, and they should all be able to gain Nibbana simply by developing compassion. However, compassion alone is not sufficient to gain Sotapanna.

An ordinary person can understand Dhamma within ordinary understanding. Subject to individual differences, an ordinary person may think that Buddha's Dhamma is a life style. Subject to individual differences, an ordinary person not knowing four-fold Nibbana may speak of Dhamma that they haven't realized for themselves by dividing the teachings of the Buddha. Instead of giving priority to Buddha and Buddha's Dhamma, they may give priority to themselves and to other ordinary Sangha members, and they may talk about personal stories and others subject matters during the time that is allocated for their Dhamma discussions pretending to be disciples of Buddha, but they are not disciples of Buddha. In this manner, the path that leads to Buddha's perfect Dhamma may seem to have disappeared in the absence of Arahants.

One way to understand an ordinary practitioner is to identify the extent to which they divide Buddha's Dhamma that is universally applicable as a socially made division, tradition, and consciously produced meditation practice. Nibbana cannot be socially produced. Nibbana cannot be produced through concentration alone by ignoring the aspect of karma and noble order, Nibbana happens in its own time like birth and death for beings shaped by one's own karma and merits.

Chapter Fifteen:

Practical Middle Way

Middle mind training is very practical, and it allows a person to practice within the usual activities, because it is within activities that a person can do and maintain mindfulness. When a person is going and doing the usual activities which allow a person to maintain mindfulness, such mindfulness can be developed to gain right mindfulness by applying wisdom based on Buddha's Dhamma in daily life. In that way, Buddha's Dhamma is perfect, as it allows integrating Dhamma into a person's daily activities so that a person's daily activities can become a place where a person can apply Dhamma practice.

To a great extent, understanding truth will allow one to prolong happiness gained through worldly experience. In general, people tend to suffer when they are unable to let go of things that they are making up in their minds. What a person is thinking may not be what is happening. When this occurs, it becomes a delusion. Something that is not the truth can cause suffering. While ordinary, a practitioner may develop noble mindfulness in this manner; the practice of noble mindfulness (right mindfulness) requires one to think and focus on one's thoughts to think beyond ordinary ways, which one can do within daily activities.

Noble mindfulness can be developed by maintaining mindfulness towards one's own thoughts and choosing to do good and avoid bad within daily activities. For example, a mind can make up a past when the past is gone, and, at times, thoughts can pass on without a person noticing them. Whether a person recognizes such thoughts or not, they can produce or prolong sufferings. Instead, to develop a noble path, if a person can watch over the person's own mind and thoughts and choose to do good and avoid bad, this will be a way to develop noble mindfulness to reduce stress. For example, when thoughts making up a past bring up sufferings, a person can do wholesome things, such as picking up from thoughts anything that needs resolving, and attempt to resolve things that need resolving and avoid unwholesome things that bring stress. In that sense, unwholesomeness is clinging to things that are gone, as they are gone, and it is meaningless to worry about such things excessively. Letting go of things that are gone will allow a person to gain peace of mind, middle-way practice, a step come closer to the realization of truth, and walk the noble path towards Sotapanna.

One technique that can be used to reduce self-view is trying to be happy with things as they are . When these habits develop within a person, ordinary ways can't seem to get enough of worldly experiences in one's mind and tend to feel and say in one's mind, "not enough". They tend to feel too upset when faced with difficulties in life (thinking that's not ok), instead letting go of things that are gone, doing what is needed to be done while resolve things, you can reduce clinging to self-view. These techniques that allow a person to deal better with life difficulties are particularly useful when circumstances are not favourable. Too much sadness can sometimes paralyse a person in mind to the extent that sometimes people may struggle to do things that they need to do. In this manner, applying wisdom, reducing clinging to self-view will allow a person to focus more on resolving things rather than worrying too much about such things in one's mind.

Similarly, the way of letting go of self-others and the world is also a practice in thoughts, a subjective process. In this manner, doing things that are beneficial without keeping too many expectations is a noble way of doing. For example, if a student puts all efforts to preparing an exam without keeping too many expectations either to pass or to fail, that will help the student to succeed and keep worries down at the same time.

Instead of positive and negative thinking, if a person is told that there are two sides in life that are possible and that uncertainty is a way of life and that ups and downs are what are usual, this will help the person to deal better with life experiences. Therefore, reducing expectations and just doing things that are beneficial will allow a person to extend happiness coming through worldly experiences.

In that sense, middle way training is very practical. For instance, getting too upset, too worried about self, others and the world can produce depression, anxiety, addictions and similar things, and giving up on self physically or emotionally can harm a person. Quitting an ordinary world and conventions are not practical and feasible, as wherever one goes, whether in the forest or in the town, whatever role one plays, whether it's living as a monk based on conventions, a householder based on conventions, a friend based on conventions or a parent based on conventions, given that the ordinary world we live in is filled with conventions, one only gets to live with conventions. Either in the forest or in the town, both are still conventions. Instead, middle way shows how a person can find inner satisfaction while living with conventions in an ordinary world by giving up clinging to such conventions in the person's mind.

Chapter Sixteen:

Understanding Conventions

A person may develop a habit of touching the worldly experiences based on conventions in mind since a birth. Getting attached to self-view developed based on conventions is the common way. Conventions are socially agreed ways of doing things including concepts, languages, rituals, lifestyles, social identities and social divisions, they are conventions. Common ways of thinking based on conventions make a person experience eight worldly conditions: happiness, and sadness, losses and gains, and similar experiences. Information coming from sensory information are interpreted based on conventions and common ways that what a person learns since childhood. Since birth, people construct self-view (others and the world) based on conventions and conventions refers to things that are commonly accepted and practiced among the people across societies. An individual derives an understanding of self (*who am I?, where did I come from?...*) based on conventions.

Almost all practitioners are aware that abandoning self-view is an important aspect in Buddha's Dhamma as a way of gaining satisfaction and reducing clinging to worldly life. But most practitioners do not seem to know how to abandon self-view in practice. There is a path (four stages) and practice (practice to reach each stage) to reaching Nibbana.

The next obvious question is how can a person abandon self-view and clinging to social practices/rituals?

Understanding how people construct self-view will make it easier for a wise person to give up clinging to self-view. After being born into the world, based on sensory information and on what others say (social learning), a person constructs an understanding of self based on conventions. Conventions are agreed to by people across societies, such as languages, social practices, rituals, social identities, social roles, etc. Based on social practices and social roles, in mind and in thoughts, a person constructs various things, such as various social roles. The mind changes its construct so that, from role to role, from time to time and situation to situation, the mind constructs an understanding of self, others and the world based on conventional ways, and conventions are subject to change. Consequently, as thoughts come and go, sensory experiences are subject to change. If a person tries to grab hold of changing things, a person's effort to hold tight to worldly things will be in vain, because the person will not be able to retain worldly experiences and conventions with stability, and the attempt will prove fruitless and will produce mental sufferings to the person so that clinging to self-view will be the extent of the person's mental suffering.

In reality, since thoughts function without a person's control, clinging to such thoughts that are inevitably changing as belonging to the person can produce stress when they change in ways that the person does not want. In this manner, dissatisfaction coming from worldly life and the sufferings and self-view of a person occur due to the erroneous understanding that there is a stable self rather than understanding that things related to self are inevitably changing. A wise ordinary person can learn to experience both the ups and downs of life with equanimity within daily life, instead of worrying too much over things that a person is unable to change. Letting go of things that are possible to do in the best possible ways within one's daily life is a wise thing to do.

A person who struggles to maintain a harmony between thoughts, words and actions by clinging to worldly experience will struggle to find inner peace. Instead, if a person tries to balance thoughts, speech and action to reduce clinging to self-view and conventions within daily life, the person will find more peace and harmony within. To bring out such a practice, one needs to be honest to oneself and take self-responsibility to do good for self, others and the world by avoiding bad (clinging to self-view and conventions) as much as possible within one's daily life. Those who pretend to have gained Nibbana and are giving instructions to others how to become enlightened without gaining enlightenment for themselves are going to put themselves at a loss. They will not only prevent others from reaching Nibbana but prevent themselves from gaining the benefit of a Dhamma practice. Instead, ordinary practitioners can develop their ordinary practices to understand the teachings beyond ordinary ways and conventions by hearing from Arahants. The self knows all about it, which is why Buddha's Dhamma is always a self-declaration, and self-declaring should follow up with reasoning, so that a person should be able to explain fourfold Nibbana with reasoning (i.e., for example, Nibbana is not a meditation practice or sharing personal stories, etc. because Nibbana is a personal experience just like ups and downs for each person), without expecting anything from others. If a wise practitioner can recognise the words of Arahants (and not the external appearance or conventions), they can recognize and understand Buddha's Dhamma and Nibbana.

Typically, in ordinary life, people are more likely to accept things that are commonly accepted as good things, such as gains and wins, and are less willing to accept things that are commonly accepted as bad things, such as losses, etc. This is because they have an underlying tendency to think that bad things should not or cannot happen to them. Yet, in reality, all people must experience good and bad things, ups and downs in life, all of which are subjective experiences for each person.

Based on conventions and sensory information that involve hearing or seeing and similar things that are constantly changing and are experienced by a person, which are worldly experiences that are constantly changing, a person will construct a world with an underlying tendency to believe that the world is a stable place. When the experience of that world is touched by ups and downs, a person with an underlying tendency to believe that there is a stable self and a stable world is more likely to experience distress. In this manner, a person constructs not only views of self, others and the world but also distress that comes with such things in one's thoughts blocking worldly satisfaction due to an erroneous understanding of life. Instead, by understanding life and the mind, a person can let go of mental sufferings to make the most of worldly life and gain satisfaction within one's daily life.

A person who has an underlying tendency to believe they are stable as people ("me, myself, and I"), as well as others and the world based on conventions, is more likely to experience distress when they experience instabilities and changes that impact their understanding of self, such as illnesses, death, loss of things that are important for self, and changes happening in others who they think are stable and the worldly experiences that belong to them. Yet, in reality, irrespective of the underlying tendencies of a person's belief or the tendency to accept, all people who are born are faced with ups and downs and will experience death.

An ordinary practitioner can reduce mental sufferings by allowing the practitioners to see the truth, wake up to reality and see the true-life experience in daily life to let go of mental sufferings that come from clinging to self-view and conventions. If the person combines giving up clinging to self-view while attending to those who have given up fetters, as a consequence, Nibbana will come to the person on its own time.

If an ordinary practitioner will understand these words and will give priority to the words in their lives, that person will apply Dhamma in the person's own life and will come a step close to gaining Nibbana.

Chapter Seventeen:

Living Without Touching the Earth

Thinking that happiness and joy gained out of worldly experiences can last forever, an ordinary person touches the world in mind since birth, liking and disliking worldly experiences too much again and again. As joy and pleasures arise from worldly experiences, liking them too much, a person may expect to experience more and more joys and pleasures through worldly life. Yet, changes happen to joys and pleasures experienced through worldly life; joys can turn into sorrow, and pleasures can turn in to displeasures. Often, it is the same thing you liked the most that produce the most mental pain when it changes. In this manner, based on common ways of thinking, an ordinary person (since birth everyone walks in this path) may initially be baffled and experience disbelief or shock when forced to experience changing worldly experiences in life. Life experience can vary from trauma to relationship issues, to financial struggles, to illnesses, to the death of a close associate and various other difficult worldly experiences including social economic pressures. Yet, based on personal life experiences, if a person comes to understand without a doubt that worldly life and common ways of think indeed bring mental pain, thus grasping changes is meaningless, because they are going to change anyway. Instead, making the most of them is a wise thing to do. In this manner, awakening to truth means understanding life experiences with wisdom to a greater extent.

Based on one's personal life experiences, if someone endures various kinds of worldly hardships and understands for themselves that life is not easy, that is the kind of an understanding that helps an ordinary practitioner want to practice middle mind training. At the next level, if an ordinary person understands that grasping worldly life can without a doubt produce mental pain, and it's not worth the pain, that kind of understanding helps an ordinary practitioner to continue training in the middle path. Otherwise, one may just hear and talk about the path and live a lifestyle without necessarily applying the middle path training. Thus, practicing Dhamma for an ordinary practitioner means applying Dhamma to oneself, and, as the result of applying Dhamma practice, should reduce one's pride, greediness, and extreme sadness towards worldly experiences. If these things are not reduced, it is unreasonable to say that one has practiced Dhamma despite one's years in meditation practice.

Thinking that it is possible to retain stability in self and worldly experiences, a person may develop a habit of touching the worldly experiences too much in mind since birth. You may take common ways of thinking as an accurate reflection of truth or reality. Yet, when changes happen in self and worldly experiences, the way you are thinking based on common ways may not match the true-life experiences. When the things that happen in life don't align with what you are thinking, and when what you were expecting to experience is not what is happening in life, you can feel dissatisfaction.

The ordinary way of thinking is what is common, what is common is what is socially created, what is socially created does not align with things that happen in a person's life based on universal ways; birth, death, illnesses and ups and downs that everyone experiences in worldly life. Self-view and social divisions are socially created constructs. What is socially constructed is not given a value or importance by the universe and its way of functioning. All beings regardless of their social identities and divisions must experience birth, death, ups and downs at random times. Thus, common ways of thinking that are socially created have limitations; such thinking does not align with a person's true-life experiences.

It is universally applicable for everyone that whatever they have is subject to change and that, when changes happen to worldly experiences, certain changes can bring mental sufferings. It is universally applicable is that mental pain can be reduced by understanding true life experiences; life has both ups and downs and natural and universal functioning. Mental pain can be reduced by reducing mental attachment to changing worldly experiences within daily life.

Chapter Eighteen:

The Direct Practice: Stream Entry

In Buddha's training path, there is a direct path that allows a person a way to gain Stream Entry, which is by abandoning the fetters, self-view through middle mind training and developing confirmed confidence in the Triple Gem. The practice to develop the direct path is letting go of worldly attachment by reducing clinging to ways in which one creates, maintains and strengthens self-view, along with social practices and doubts which maintain and strengthen self-view by understanding and developing confirmed confidence in Buddha and Buddha's Dhamma by hearing from Arahants and applying the Dhamma to one's daily life.

If one can reduce self-clinging and clinging to social practices and develop confirmed confidence in the Triple Gem, one can gain Stream Entry and above. On the other hand, if one is unable to give up clinging excessively to self-view, social practices and develop confirmed confidence, one is unlikely to gain Nibbana despite the long term (or short term) practicing of meditation, lifestyles and rituals. In other words, when the direct path is not followed, the ancient path to Nibbana can be prevented, and when the direct path is followed, a person will be able to gain Nibbana.

Buddha's Dhamma always lies beyond ordinary ways. For example, ordinary ways of life and worldly life are created when a person has too many likes and too much dislike towards what they experience about themselves, others and the world based on sensory information that comes and goes in one's mind and thoughts. Given that things on earth are always changing, when a person's worldly experience changes, a person can experience ongoing stress when changes happen, especially when changes happen in the way the person does not desire. Therefore, when a person touches the earth in the person's mind, and when experiencing worldly experiences meaning likes and dislikes and expectations towards what the person creates as self, others and the world in the absence of permanent self, others and the world, there is a possibility that the person can get hurt, because made up things don't last long. In Buddha's training path and the noble path, reducing liking to gain Stream Entry does not mean giving up people by ignoring them as applicable for oneself rather treating them with care while they are still there knowing that they can change for various reasons including natural death or separation, as these things are a part of life for all of us. Similarly, reducing liking in Buddha's path does not mean no longer doing things for others rather fulfilling responsibilities towards others without expecting anything from others as a way of living that one needs to adopt to develop the noble path and the noble way of living. In this manner, one does not hurt oneself or others. When a person knows for sure that the person has done everything good and beneficial to the person's level best and reduces expectations, understands how the universe functions to bring good and bad, and duality, how society functions, and what others think and do not think, these things will not bother a person who truly follows Dhamma in life. In that sense, Dhamma protects a person who follows Dhamma from worldly experiences by reducing suffering and bringing wellbeing. On the other hand, if Dhamma is not followed and instead ritual, religion, division, tradition, and lifestyle are followed without abandoning the fetters, the same benefit cannot be expected. In this manner, Buddha's Dhamma and the direct path refers to abandoning clinging too much to the self-view, social practices, and doubts while developing the confirmed confidence in the Triple Gem. In this manner, Buddha's Dhamma is perfect, as it protects one from hurting oneself and others. Therefore, an ordinary practitioner will be able to reduce suffering by reducing self-clinging and clinging to social practices by following the middle way within daily life, while attending to Triple Gem to gain good things in life, after life and Nibbana.

Concluding Remarks

What is universally applicable for everyone is that whatever they have are subject to change. What is universally applicable is that when changes happening to worldly experiences, certain changes can bring mental sufferings. What is universally applicable is that mental pain can be reduced by understanding true life experience; life has both ups and downs; natural and universal functioning and by reducing mental attachment to changing worldly experiences within daily life. It has often been claimed that, to practice Dhamma in real life, one must give up worldly matters. However, giving up worldly matters indicates realizing that worldly matters are not permanent; they are subject to change and that worldly matters are non-self. Giving up worldly matters to practice Dhamma does not indicate that one must give up worldly matters physically, because the physical world is created in the mind, and it is the giving up in the mind or non-attachment that is emphasized here. Therefore, those who practice middle way training is expected to grow in all areas of life, both materialistically and spiritually.

Similarly, by understanding that self-view is strengthened by social practices, that certain ways of doing things in societies can divide people, and that certain social practices can put pressure on people and affect their wellbeing, one with wisdom will likely want to but be free from the need to give too much value to social practices (rituals and life styles) and instead become a good person true to one's own heart and do good to others by fulfilling responsibilities without expecting anything from others. This can produce inner satisfaction and mental peace. For example, standard ways of doing things and social practices make it a norm to become sad when losing things and become happy when gaining things. Similarly, it seems that society can sometimes portray that one can have a perfect life, perfect relationship, perfect household, perfect school grades, and a perfect job and similar ways. Yet, in real life, it is not always possible to have perfect things, and this is something one gets to learn from one's own life experience, a realization. When the real-life experiences fail to meet what one expects to experience in one's mind, one can feel disappointed. Therefore, by understanding that grasping earthly things too much can bring stress to oneself, a wise person will likely want to let go of clinging to earthly experiences including social practices and rituals.

Similarly, a mind can possess the desire for physical/material things even in the absence of the same things. A mind can project past and future events in the absence of the past and future. Similarly, a mind can project self-view and others even in the absence of a permanent self and others. Therefore, in Buddha's training path, letting go refers to giving up getting attached to one's mind and one's thoughts but not giving up physical/material things. Materials things are needed for survival, and everyone in Buddha's path is encouraged to provide those things. For one who has given up liking and disliking materials in mind, the presence of materials remains empty.

Middle mind training can be applied to let go of self-view. For example, when faced with duality in one's life, by not becoming too sad and too happy and similar ways, one can reduce grasping self-view and retaining satisfaction in daily life. Letting go of things can be facilitated by giving up desires to experience certain things and not experiencing (middle-way) certain things. The path leading to Nibbana and Buddha's teachings of letting go across four stages becomes a comfortable middle way and practical thing to do. For example, at the Sotapanna level, a person may still seek amusement in the same way as the vast majority of people (ordinary people). By simply cutting off the stressful side and experiencing sensual pleasures, a Sotapanna may gain amusement in traveling, graduating, even by posting pictures of themselves on Facebook, and taking selfies and similar things in both monastic and non-monastic settings, as the setting is not relevant to one's training in mind Nibbana. Having cut off both amusement and non-amusement, at the Arahant stage, one will do the above things only if they benefit others. Each stage of Nibbana differs. Nibbana is a blissful experience for Sotapanna.

From a practice point of view, those who hear Dhamma and are talking about Dhamma but are not applying Dhamma to themselves are practicing in a way in which gaining Nibbana is not possible. Those who hear Dhamma and understand Dhamma beyond ordinary views to let go of such practices by applying Dhamma to themselves are practicing in the correct way to gain Nibbana. Those who's pride disappeared and those who have completed four-fold Nibbana have completed their practice in the right manner. Ideally, one should complete four-fold Nibbana before telling others, because interpreting Buddha' words and teachings in a wrong manner can prevent Nibbana for many.

In contemporary times, there is a higher probability that an average person will get to hear Dhamma only as a religion, a ritual, a lifestyle, a division, a meditation practice (living in the present moment and being aware) from ordinary Dhamma teachers. Ordinary views that are preliminary practices before Stream Entry are widespread across societies. Yet, at the same time, it appears that ordinary views alone can prevent Nibbana for many practitioners in the absence of Arahants. Opportunities to hear the teachings of Buddha from an Arahant are rare. Given that Nibbana is about letting go in phases, one who wishes to gain Nibbana will benefit if one learns to let go of the preliminary practices, such as grasping at a religion, a lifestyle, rituals, meditation practices and similar things to gain Stream Entry. A wise practitioner will benefit by letting go of preliminary practices to think beyond standard ways.

One can learn to give up these preliminary practices by understanding that Nibbana is universally applicable, and the practice is the same for all.

The noble path and noble ariyan way of doing things always lies beyond ordinary ways of doing things. Below are some of examples. Instead of dividing and hurting others and hurting self, the ariyan way of living is to treat everyone with genuine care.

Training in the noble path requires one to understand universal truth: stress that is created due to duality and karma and the Triple Gem.

These days, it appears that practitioners tend to give priority to meditation practices including mindfulness meditation. Yet, meditation practices, such as maintaining bare attention, can be subject to change. For example, a person may gain temporary relief during a meditation practice only to lose that relief when the person comes out of the meditation practice.

Nibbana is not a conscious process of observing thoughts but a process of natural detachment that happens across four stages shaped by one's karma and merits.

By understanding that Nibbana is not man-made, a wise practitioner will benefit by understanding universally applicable teachings, Nibbana. For example, birth, death, illnesses, and natural disasters are universal happenings; they are a part of life for all beings. Similarly, duality and karma are universally applicable to all beings. To be free from worldly experiences, karma, and samsara, one needs to let go of ordinary views and practices. The practice one can adapt to let go of things requires middle mind training and developing merits.

Wisdom, merits, and Nibbana are linked. The universal law of karma always applies to all beings. Thus, the practice leading to Nibbana always begins by refuge in Triple Gem. Those who attend Buddha and Arahants will gain higher wisdom, genuine care, and merits that are needed for good things in life and Nibbana.

References

Dhammatalks.org.
https://www.dhammatalks.org

SuttaCentral.net.
https://suttacentral.net

SuttaFriends.org
https://suttafriends.org

www.ingramcontent.com/pod-product-compliance
Lightning Source LLC
LaVergne TN
LVHW041629070526
838199LV00052B/3293